THE GREAT ARTISTS
& THEIR WORLD
MICHELANGELO

NEW
FOREST
PRESS

Publisher: Melissa Fairley
Editor: Guy Croton
Designer: Carol Davis
Production Controller: Ed Green
Production Manager: Suzy Kelly

ISBN: 978-1-84898-309-0
Library of Congress Control Number: 2010925210
Tracking number: nfp0004

North American edition copyright © TickTock Entertainment Ltd. 2010
First published in North America in 2010 by New Forest Press,
PO Box 784, Mankato, MN 56002
www.newforestpress.com

Printed in the USA
9 8 7 6 5 4 3 2 1

Every effort has been made to trace the copyright holders, and we apologize in advance for any omissions.
We would be pleased to insert the appropriate acknowledgments in any subsequent edition of this publication.

The author has asserted his right to be identified as the author of this book in
accordance with the Copyright, Design, and Patents Act, 1988.

CONTENTS

INTRODUCTION

Often named as the greatest artist that ever lived, Michelangelo di Lodovico Buonarroti Simoni (1475–1564) was a painter, sculptor, architect, draughtsman, and poet. One of the most famous of all artists, he is usually known simply by his first name and over the course of his 88 years, he changed western art beyond compare.

EARLY TRAINING

Although he grew up to be one of the greatest artists in history, with outstanding skills and vast knowledge, as a boy Michelangelo did not like school. Despite his father's exasperation, he left school early and at the age of thirteen, became an apprentice in the workshop of the successful fresco painter Domenico Ghirlandaio (1449–94). Ghirlandaio taught him the basics of fresco painting, but within a year, the ruler of Florence, Lorenzo de' Medici, invited him to become his guest. In the large Medici household, he studied Lorenzo's collection of classical Greek and Roman sculpture and he was taught sculpture by Bertoldo di Giovanni, a former assistant of Donatello. He also came in contact with some of the most learned men of the times and inspired by these intellectuals, he learned to speak and write well. The powerful "Lorenzo the Magnificent" became his first patron and he soon traveled to Bologna and Rome where he studied antique buildings and sculpture and received several more commissions.

RENAISSANCE MAN

By the fifteenth century, parts of Italy, such as Florence and Rome, had become extremely important cultural centers of Europe with new ideas, inventions, and reforms developing in science, the arts, and the humanities. It was believed that classical culture was better than contemporary culture and this revival later became known as the Renaissance, which means "rebirth." Although as a boy Michelangelo had not been interested in academic study, as he grew up, surrounded by these developments, mixing with the scholars in the Medici household, and studying the arts, his creative and intellectual development increased beyond anything his father had expected. He and Leonardo da Vinci are known as "polymaths"—people who are experts in several different areas—and this is also what is meant by the term "Renaissance man."

"IL DIVINO"

Michelangelo was a prolific worker. The range and scale of his production was vast, from his huge statue of David in Florence, to his paintings on the ceiling of the Sistine Chapel, to the design of the dome of St. Peter's Basilica in Rome. He also left many eloquent and expressive drawings, poems, and letters. Even though Leonardo and Raphael were also alive, from his mid-thirties, most people believed Michelangelo to be the greatest living artist and he became known as "Il divino Michelangelo," which meant just what it seems—the divine Michelangelo. (He was 23 years younger than Leonardo and eight years older than Raphael and he lived longer than both of them). He was the first artist to have two biographies of himself published while he was alive.

Because he was such a productive and determined worker, Michelangelo's often arrogant manner earned him another unique description. He was energetic, passionate, ambitious, and awe-inspiring with an incredible memory and people described his attitude as his *terribilità*, which can be translated as "terrifying power." He certainly must have seemed frighteningly commanding, proud, and imposing as he took on such huge and difficult commissions and accomplished everything so well, but he was also vulnerable, anxious, and often miserable. Despite his fame and wealth, at many points in his life, he believed he was a failure and in particular, spent years sorrowing over the colossal tomb he was originally asked to create for Pope Julius II, but which Julius himself and then later popes told him to abandon.

LEGACY

Much of Michelangelo's life remains a mystery, but his work continues to inspire and amaze. Accepted as one of the most inspirational, original, and talented artists in history, an enormous number of artists have since attempted to imitate his ideas, techniques, and dynamic style. Working at a time when art and culture were changing dramatically, he helped to make the Renaissance a time of remarkable achievement. The first movement that followed him was Mannerism, which developed directly from his style, but nearly five centuries after his death, his enormous influence on art continues.

THE WORLD IN THE 1500S

Although the year 1500 seems today to be a very long time ago, historians use this date to mark the beginning of what is referred to as "modern history." It is an arbitrary date but it does mark the change between the medieval world and the "modern" world whose values continue today. The "High Renaissance" to which Michelangelo belonged, dates from about the year 1500, and was the high point of a change in European history that started about one hundred years earlier in Italy. Renaissance means rebirth, and refers to a return to the classical ideals of the ancient Greeks and Romans. The Renaissance was characterized by an increasing independence of thought, which led to the shattering of traditional Christian unity as well as a new curiosity about the world in which people found themselves. The voyages of Columbus opened up the "New World" of Central and South America to ruthless exploitation by the Spanish and Portuguese, who were to follow. Islam spread rapidly through the empires of Africa, a country shrouded in mystery to the Europeans who had begun to establish trading stations on Africa's West coast. Trade routes were becoming established throughout the world, linking the Americas, Europe, India, Asia, and Africa, bringing wealth to new dynasties and changing the lives of millions of people.

THE GREAT AND HIDDEN CONTINENT

Africa was cut off from European explorers by the Saharan desert, until the maritime nations such as Portugal started trading with West African kingdoms such as Benin. It was from this time that the slave trade began to grow.

RELIGIOUS REVOLUTION

Martin Luther was a German monk who demanded the reform of the Catholic Church, which he saw as corrupt. His followers, the reformers, started a movement which became known as the Reformation. In 1521, Luther was expelled from the Church because of his protests. He set up his own movement which became known as the Protestant Church.

THE POWER OF THE CROWN

Nowhere was the growing power of the monarchy more clearly felt than in England. European countries developed ideas of nationhood ruled by kings who had absolute power over their people. The French kings were portrayed as Roman emperors: "Kings by the grace of God, not by election or force." The maritime empires of Spain and Portugal were becoming established and were to dominate world trade during the course of the 16th century. Henry VIII, King of England from 1509 to 1547, challenged the power of the Church of Rome by establishing a new Church in England. In 1533, Henry became "Supreme Head of the Church of England."

SPREADING THE WORD

The development of the printing press in the 16th century permitted the rapid spread of ideas and had a profound impact on society. Gutenberg's printing process developed in the 15th century caused a growing revolution as numerous identical copies of words and pictures could be made quickly and cheaply. One example of the impact of printing was that people no longer depended upon one interpretation of the Scriptures, but could study them for themselves.

THE PROGRESS OF SCIENCE

The sciences advanced faster in the 16th century than they had at any point in history. The study of natural sciences became systematic and based on investigation such as Vesalius's first exact descriptions of the human body. Leonardo da Vinci formed theories about the circulation of the blood and made detailed anatomical studies of the human form in a true spirit of enquiry.

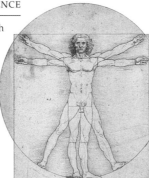

A NEW VIEW OF THE WORLD IN ABOUT 1508

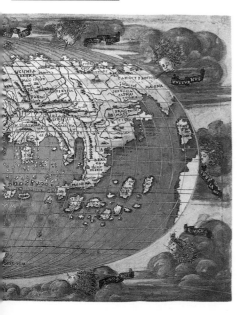

COPERNICUS

The Polish monk Copernicus proved that the Earth turned about the Sun rather than the Sun about the Earth. This discovery was so revolutionary at a time when everyone believed that the Earth was at the center of the Universe, that he was terrified of making his discovery known.

THE WORLD OF MICHELANGELO

Michelangelo was born on March 6, 1475, in Caprese, a small town north of Arezzo, but moved to Florence with his family when barely a month old. It was a time of great change in Italy, which was made up of small states continually struggling for more power and territory. Most of the inhabitants depended on the land for their livelihood. The one means of fast progression was through the all-powerful Church of Rome, which offered a means of escape from the drudgery of peasant life. Michelangelo benefited greatly from the patronage of the Church and received all of his greatest commissions from Church sources. However, the great upheavals in the Church during Michelangelo's lifetime were a result of the deep corruption that had grown unchecked over many years. Italy suffered devastation at the hands of invading armies at the turn of the century, the French invading in 1494, when Michelangelo was 19 years old, the Spanish taking Rome in 1527. These great upheavals must have affected Michelangelo as they did so many of his fellow countrymen and women.

LORENZO THE MAGNIFICENT

The Medici family were enormously powerful and rich, making their money in banking and exerting their power by ruling Florence for over 300 years. Lorenzo de' Medici, who was in power at the time Michelangelo was growing up in Florence, owned a collection of fragments of antique sculpture made up of broken pillars and stone figures which were kept in the garden of San Marco. Lorenzo de' Medici allowed artists to study the antique sculptures, including, it would seem, the young Michelangelo who was allowed to work there staying in the Medici household. Lorenzo de' Medici undoubtedly saw great talent in Michelangelo and helped his career as an artist. Lorenzo died in 1492, and was succeeded by his son Pier de'Medici, continuing the family line.

THE LEARNED ARCHITECT

The buildings of Donato Bramante displayed great learning and knowledge of the classical builders of antiquity. His buildings, such as the famous church of St. Peter's in Rome, were originally designed to compete with the famous ancient ruins such as the Pantheon, but Bramante's designs were too extravagant for the Church's purse. Nevertheless, the harmonious classical forms of his buildings such as the Tempietto in Rome embody the Renaissance ideals of order and symmetry. Michelangelo praised Bramante saying he was *"... as worthy an architect as any since ancient times."*

ISABELLA D'ESTE

Isabella d'Este was a woman of great learning who became a patron of the Renaissance arts, employing people such as the artist Correggio and the writer Baldassare Castiglione whose books popularized Humanist philosophy. Humanism, led by the Dutch philosopher Erasmus, was an important movement of the Renaissance. Its central belief was that human reason was more important than religious doctrine and, like other Renaissance movements, referred back to classical studies. Isabella d'Este's fame in Italy is evident by the number of portraits that exist by artists such as Leonardo da Vinci and this one by Titian.

SNOWMAN

It is said that Lorenzo the Magnificent's son, Pier de' Medici, did not recognize the value of the creative genius of Michelangelo as his father had, and the story goes that in frivolous mood Pier ordered Michelangelo to make a snowman in the courtyard of the Medici palace. From this moment Michelangelo realized his future might be better— and safer— elsewhere and moved from Florence to Bologna. This move was wise for a reason Michelangelo could not have known: In 1494, Charles VIII of France with a sizeable army invaded Italy and took the city of Florence.

NICCOLO MACHIAVELLI

The Florentine statesman and political philosopher is remembered chiefly for his book written in 1532, entitled *Il Principe* (The Prince). This study of political power concluded that those in power must be prepared to do bad things if they judge that good will follow. His name has become associated with political deviousness but that is largely the result of subsequent criticism by the Church.

THE ART OF HIS DAY

The Renaissance was a rebirth which led to new ways of thinking in the sciences, philosophy, and architecture as well as in painting and sculpture. It rejected the recent medieval past with its Gothic art and architecture, and returned to the golden ages of the great Greek and Roman civilizations. The Renaissance movement in art spanned several centuries but was at its greatest during the time of Michelangelo. The artist Giotto who lived and worked in Florence between 1267 and 1337, is today known as the "father" of Western painting because of his method of representing figures and landscapes with greater realism and in a more naturalistic style.

Giotto's influence on later painters, particularly Masaccio, carried forward the sculptural realism and solidity of form, which exemplifies Renaissance painting and which can be seen to culminate in the figures of Michelangelo.

BRONZE PUTTO

Andrea del Verrocchio

Renaissance art often included naked children with wings, depicting cupids and angels. This was a fashion borrowed from the ancient Greeks and Romans. Putto is Italian for little boy. The plural is putti.

CRUCIFIXION

Matthias Grünewald

Although painted at the same time as Raphael's *School of Athens*, the difference in artistic approach to the paintings could not have been greater. Matthias Grünewald was a German contemporary of Raphael who ignored the influence of the Renaissance, choosing a deeply religious theme and working in a way that bears a greater resemblance to the medieval Gothic style filled with darkness and suffering. The painting was commissioned by the Antonite monastery hospital at Isenheim near Strasbourg, which cared for plague victims. The intention of the painting is to give comfort to the dying by reinforcing their religious faith; Grünewald portrays Christ's body covered by sores because he felt this would help the plague victims to relate Christ's situation to their own.

THE SCHOOL OF ATHENS

Raphael

Raphael was working in Florence at the same time as Michelangelo and Leonardo, but his career was cut short by his death in 1520, when he was 37 years old. In his lifetime Raphael was considered to be an artist of equal stature to both Michelangelo and Leonardo despite being the youngest—31 years younger than Leonardo. Raphael's great achievement was to create harmonious compositions including figures who appear to be full of graceful movement. When Raphael was 25 years old, he was commissioned by Pope Julius II to decorate the room in the Vatican named the Stanza della Segnatura. In true Renaissance tradition this fresco is dedicated to the great classical philosophers. At the center of the painting stand Plato and Aristotle; portrayed around them are Ptolemy, Euclid, Pythagoras, Socrates, and more.

THE VIRGIN ON THE ROCKS

Leonardo da Vinci

One of the most famous names in the history of art, Leonardo da Vinci, was a contemporary of Michelangelo. Leonardo's interests spread far beyond painting. His notebooks reveal the extent of his interests, including sketches of mechanical inventions such as tanks and even helicopters. He wrote a treatise on painting which described perspective and how to use an artistic device known as *trompe l'oeil* (pictures that deceive the eye).

DETAIL FROM THE BIRTH OF VENUS *Sandro Botticelli*

Painted in Michelangelo's home town of Florence in 1484, Sandro Botticelli's famous painting caused a sensation because it was an important commission which chose to deal with a mythological rather than a religious subject. It deals with one of the Renaissance's favorite subjects, classical mythology, depicting the birth of the goddess Venus. Botticelli represents Venus as an ideal of classical female beauty. Renaissance artists began to idealize the model. They used an imagined type of model formed from classical statues and "improved" on nature rather than representing it.

FAMILY, FRIENDS, & OTHERS

THE FEATURES OF MICHELANGELO

The *Pietà* of 1550, made when Michelangelo was 75 years old, is actually a "deposition" that refers to the taking down of the dead Christ from the cross. The cowled head of Nicodemus, who is said to have carried Christ's body, is thought to be sculpted on Michelangelo's own features.

Detail of the Pietà.

Michelangelo was the second of five sons born to Lodovico and Francesca Buonarroti. The 490 surviving letters that Michelangelo wrote over the course of his nearly 90 years to his family, friends, and patrons, provide a valuable insight into the life of Michelangelo and of Renaissance Italy. When Michelangelo was in Rome in 1509, he corresponded with his father over money matters—his parents had begun to depend upon Michelangelo's income —and his brothers' careers. In June 1509, he wrote: *"Dearest father. I realize from your last letter how things are going there and how Giovansimone is behaving... I thought I had arranged matters for them, namely how they might hope to set up a good workshop with my help, as I promised them, and in this hope might apply themselves to becoming proficient and learning their trade, so as to be able to run the shop when the time came."* Michelangelo wrote to his wayward brother the same month:

"Giovansimone. They say that if you treat a good man kindly you make him even better, and if you treat a wicked man so you make him worse... I am not saying you are wicked, but the way you are carrying on, you never ever please me, or the others. Let me tell you that you have nothing of your own in this world, and your spending money and your home expenses are what I give you. If I hear anything more about the way you behave, I'll ride with the post all the way to Florence to show you your mistake..."

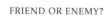

FRIEND OR ENEMY?

Raphael of Urbino was a contemporary of Michelangelo who learned a great deal from the master. There was some rivalry between them. Michelangelo is reported to have said that all the misunderstandings he had with Pope Julius II were as a result of the envy of Raphael and Bramante. However, Raphael was a great admirer of Michelangelo's art.

TRUE LOVE?

Michelangelo had many close friends but he was never married. Letters and poems written by Michelangelo show that he was very close to Tommaso Cavalieri, whom he met in Rome when he was in his fifties and Tommaso in his twenties. Tommaso was known to be an extremely handsome youth and Michelangelo was attracted by his beauty, making many drawings of him. Their friendship lasted until Michelangelo's death and Tommaso inherited many of Michelangelo's drawings, which are now lost. This drawing, entitled *Divine Head*, represents an idealized notion of beauty rather than one drawn from life, however it was made when Michelangelo first met Tommaso and may be based on his friend rather than his imagination.

FRIENDSHIP

In 1536, while he was working on the *Last Judgement* fresco in the Sistine Chapel, Michelangelo met the Marchioness of Pescara, Vittoria Colonna. Vasari tells that he: *"greatly loved the Marchioness of Pescara, with whose divine spirits he fell in love."* If Tommaso Cavalieri represented physical beauty then Vittoria, widow of the Marquis who died at the battle of Pavia 11 years earlier, represented spiritual beauty; she had devoted herself to religion after her husband's death. It is thought that the woman with the orange veil who is at the feet of Mary in the *Last Judgement* is a portrait of Vittoria. Michelangelo devoted many sonnets to Vittoria. This is an extract from "A l'alto tuo lucente diadema":

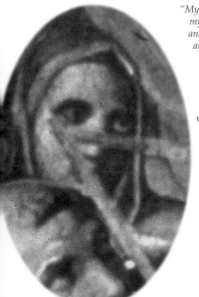

*"My strength is failing me, I spend
my breath halfway—I fall, I stray.
and yet your beauty makes me happy
and nothing else can please my heart
in love with everything sublime
but that, descending here to me
on earth, you are not set apart."*

Michelangelo was distraught when she died, forever regretting that when she was dying he did not kiss her brow or face, only her hand.

THE LIFE OF MICHELANGELO

~1475~
Michelangelo di Lodovico di Lionardo di Buonarroto Simoni (Michelangelo) born on March 6 in Caprese near Arezzo, second of five children. The family moved to Florence when Michelangelo was a month old

~1481~
Michelangelo's mother, Francesca, died when he was six years old

~1488~
Apprenticed to fresco painter Domenico Ghirlandaio in Florence for three years

~1489—1490~
Studied sculpture in the San Marco garden owned by the Medicis under Bertoldo di Giovanni. Michelangelo impressed and became acquainted with Lorenzo "The Magnificent" de' Medici

~1492~
Lorenzo de' Medici's death

~1494~
Moved to Bologna away from Pier de' Medici who had succeeded Lorenzo

~1496~
Michelangelo moved to Rome and undertook commissions. Sculpted the Pieta for Cardinal Lagraulas

~1501~
Returned to Florence which was now declared a republic

~1504~
Carved the statue of David which was installed in the main square of Florence

WHAT DO THE PAINTINGS SAY?

THE SISTINE CHAPEL CEILING

The painting of the ceiling of the Sistine Chapel in Rome is without doubt one of the greatest feats ever accomplished and this work alone is enough to have carried Michelangelo's name across the centuries as a giant among artists. The scale is breathtaking; the impact overwhelming; yet this work was accomplished by Michelangelo virtually single-handed in about four years, from 1508 to 1512. It is no wonder that Michelangelo's contemporaries called him the "divine Michelangelo." The frescoes cover approximately 622 square yards (520 square meters) across the barrel-vaulted ceiling of the barn-like building of the Chapel which stands next to the Vatican. Michelangelo was commissioned by Pope Julius II in 1505, and was given, according to the artist, a free hand to design whatever he wanted.

THE DRUNKENNESS OF NOAH

The Old Testament tells how Noah, who owned vineyards, became drunk and lay naked. His son Ham covers his father while his brothers Japhet and Shem look away.

THE FLOOD

This panel tells the well known story of the flood, which will drown all the people, while Noah and his family climb aboard the Ark.

THE SACRIFICE

Noah built an altar in thanksgiving for being saved, and made an offering to God. God blessed Noah and his family.

The middle three panels show the Fall, Adam, and Eve:

The central area of the ceiling is made up of nine panels showing scenes from the Old Testament of the Bible, beginning with three about the Creation, three on Adam and Eve, and three on the story of Noah. They are surrounded by figures of Sibyls (prophetesses in Greek mythology) and Hebrew prophets. The design is linked by athletic male figures (ignudi) who hold bronze medallions and also serve to link the Christian stories with classical antiquity. The first three panels created by Michelangelo, deal with the story of Noah and were painted in the order shown here, although they are of course intended to be viewed in reverse starting with the Creation at the altar end of the Chapel.

THE FALL
Eve takes the apple from the serpent and Adam and Eve are expelled from the Garden of Eden.

THE CREATION OF EVE
God bids the figure of Eve arise from beside the slumbering Adam.

THE CREATION OF ADAM
This panel shows Adam just as he is about to be receive the charge of life from God.

The final three panels deal with the Creation:

GOD SEPARATING EARTH FROM WATER
The swirling, powerful figure of God creates the firmament.

THE CREATION OF THE SUN, MOON, AND STARS
An awesome, bearded God is shown in the act of creation throwing the Sun and Moon into their positions in the universe.

GOD SEPARATING LIGHT FROM DARKNESS
God cleaving the clouds of darkness, bringing forth light.

THE CREATION OF ADAM

This image is possibly one of the greatest icons of Western art. Michelangelo has depicted Adam as if just awakened and about to be charged with the energy of life through the outstretched arm of God who is borne aloft by a cloud of angels. The beginning of human history starts with this moment, captured brilliantly by Michelangelo. It is the anticipation of the moment that gives the painting its tension and vitality; Michelangelo is revealing the story to us even before it begins.

LIFE GIVING ENERGY

The eyes of Adam, God, and the angels all focus intently on the outstretched hand of God and the hand of Adam. The viewer can tell that the moment is about to happen because of the smallest of gaps which remains between the two fingers, and from the fact that Adam's hand is supine: the life-giving energy has not yet passed from one to the other.

THE BURDEN OF MORTALITY

By comparing the face of Eve before and after eating the fruit it is possible to see the consequences of her action. Her face is young and beautiful beforehand but is creased and lined with the burden of mortality as she walks away from the Garden.

THE FALL

This picture is divided into two separate scenes. The left hand scene shows Adam and Eve in the Garden of Eden. Eve reaches out behind her to take the forbidden fruit from the Tree of Knowledge, which is offered to her by the serpent. The serpent is depicted as half woman, half snake, and reflects the male dominated interpretation of the story by casting the woman in the role of temptress. The Tree of Knowledge around which the serpent is wound acts as a divide between the left hand scene and the right, which shows the expulsion of Adam and Eve from the Garden of Eden. God banishes them because having eaten of the Tree of Knowledge they know Good and Evil, and if they stay and eat of the Tree of Life they will live for ever. The angel with the sword refers to the "flaming sword" that God placed east of Eden to guard the entrance to the Garden.

STORIES FROM THE SISTINE CHAPEL

Interpretations of the ceiling frescoes differ but the subject matter may have been partly based on the decorations which were already in place when Michelangelo started his work. Michelangelo signed his contract on May 10, 1508, and was to be paid 3,000 ducats but this was quickly doubled to 6,000 ducats. Work started in July 1508 and continued until 1510 when Michelangelo traveled to Bologna, apparently to persuade the Pope to provide more money. Giorgio Vasari's *Life of Michelangelo* tells us that one day the impatient Pope asked when he would finish, to which Michelangelo replied: *"When I'm able to."* The Pope, infuriated, continued: *"You want me to have you thrown off that scaffolding now, don't you?"* The ceiling was finally completed in 1512 and unveiled on All Saints' Day. Michelangelo's letter at the time records:

"I have finished the chapel which I was painting; the Pope is very satisfied; and the other matters are not turning out as I wished but these times are very unfavorable to our art."

THE LIBYAN SIBYL

Sibyl is the Hellenistic Greek name given to a prophetess but also became linked with Old Testament prophets in Christian literature. The most famous Sibyl was Cumae (also portrayed on the Sistine ceiling), who told Aeneas in the *Aeneid* how to enter the Underworld. They are supposed to have kept in their possession books of prophecy which could be referred to in times of need. This may explain why Michelangelo depicted the Libyan Sibyl holding open a book. What the viewer sees, however, is a figure who twists to hold open the pages as she balances on tiptoe in her niche in the ceiling. Michelangelo paints the pose with breathtaking confidence and even humor; the Sibyl's dress is caught under the block of stone on which she balances.

DAWN AND DUSK & DAY AND NIGHT

The figures of Lorenzo and Giuliano sit above mythological figures who rest upon the sarcophagi. Beneath the thoughtful Lorenzo lies the female figure of Dawn and male figure of Dusk; beneath the tense Giuliano lies the male figure of Day and female figure of Night. These represent the transient world, whereas the idealized figures of the Medicis show that they have already transcended their material life and have reached Heaven. This classical pagan symbolism mixes easily with Christian symbolism, such as the Madonna and Child to whom the men turn. The female forms are less than convincing when compared to Michelangelo's masterful handling of the male body. Nevertheless the sculptures with their complex messages about the passing of life and many details which refer to death (rams' skulls, masks, owls, moons, stars, laurels) establish Michelangelo as one of the greatest sculptors ever.

GIULIANO DE'MEDICI

Giuliano, Duke of Nemours, had died in 1516 at the age of 38. Michelangelo portrays him as alert and ready for action, in military style. He is seated with a baton across his lap, head turned, as if a commander on the point of issuing some instruction to his men.

THE MEDICI CHAPEL

The memoirs of Canon Figiovanni of San Lorenzo, Florence, record that in June 1519, Cardinal Giulio de'Medici said: *"... we are of a mind to spend about 50,000 ducats on San Lorenzo... which will be called a chapel, where there will be many tombs to bury our dead forefathers: Lorenzo, Giuliano our father, and Giuliano, and Lorenzo, brother and nephew."* In November 1519, two houses alongside the church of San Lorenzo were demolished to make room for the new chapel, and building commenced on March 1, 1520. The marble from which the tombs were to be carved was ordered from the nearby marble quarry in Carrara. The design for the chapel with its coffered dome, reflects the Pantheon which was a resting place for the famous dead of ancient Rome. Its architecture however, fuses together the accepted classical style with his own powerful invention which sometimes contradicts the old rules. Michelangelo completed only two tombs, whose carved figures on two side walls of the chapel look toward a third wall against which stands a sculpture of the Madonna and Child. Opposite the Madonna should have been a third double tomb for Lorenzo the Magnificent and his brother but work on it was abandoned in 1534, when Michelangelo left Florence for Rome.

LORENZO DE'MEDICI

Lorenzo was only 28 years old when he died in Florence in May 1519, just a few weeks after his wife had died in childbirth. Their daughter Catherine survived and eventually became Queen of France. Lorenzo was the last in the direct line of descent from Cosimo de' Medici, and it was his death that prompted the plan to build the chapel. The figure of Lorenzo is depicted with head resting on hand, as if lost in deep thought. Both Lorenzo and Giuliano are portrayed in the classical style of Roman military dress typical of Renaissance art. They are idealized, heroic figures, not true portraits. Michelangelo is reported to have said of the sculptures: *"In a thousand years' time who will care what they (Lorenzo and Giuliano) really looked like?"*

The male figure of Dusk and female figure of Dawn from Lorenzo's tomb.

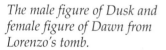

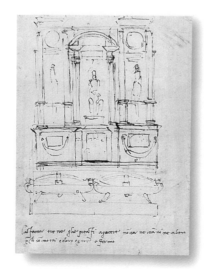

MICHELANGELO'S PLAN

This sketch with notes in Michelangelo's hand shows the planned double tomb which was to have been for Lorenzo the Magnificent and his brother.

PERSPECTIVE AND PROPORTION

The technical virtuosity of Michelangelo and his fellow artists such as Raphael and Leonardo, surpassed anything that had gone before, including the great classical Greek and Roman works that they admired so much. Representation of nature and the human form required methods to make them realistic which we take for granted today. It was not until the 1400s, that perspective was truly mastered by artists such as Uccello, creating a sense of depth within the picture. This enabled the artist to create the illusion of three dimensional objects on a two dimensional surface, such as a flat wall. Michelangelo's twisting human torsos required a complete mastery of foreshortening by which perspective is applied to a single object; an example would be a painted figure whose arm points toward the viewer showing a great deal of the hand but virtually none of the arm which is "behind" the hand.

A painter is depicted above studying the laws of foreshortening by means of thread and frame. *Woodcut by Dürer from the 1525 edition of his book on perspective and proportion.*

THE PERFECT STONE

The material favored by sculptors in Michelangelo's day was marble. This was the preferred material for carving for thousands of years and remains so today. It is a hard crystalline rock that is made from limestone and has an extremely fine texture that permits a highly polished surface. The marble quarries that supplied Michelangelo with his blocks of stone were at Carrara, on the east coast near Genoa.

A PERMANENT FINISH

The fresco method of painting was absolutely permanent because the pigments mixed with water are absorbed into the still damp surface of the wall. The colors are therefore fixed into the plaster and are less likely to suffer from superficial discoloring or damage.

HOW WERE THEY MADE?

Michelangelo's wall paintings employ a method used for hundreds of years called fresco, which is the Italian word for "fresh." Buon fresco or "true fresco" which was practiced in Italy at the time of Michelangelo was the most permanent form of wall decoration. After the wall to be painted was roughly plastered, a coat known as the arriccio was applied. It was onto this layer that the outline drawing of the final picture (known as the cartoon) was traced and so transferred to the wall. An area which could comfortably be covered by the artist in one day was then covered with another coat of plaster (intonaco), onto which the cartoon was re-drawn. The artist worked on this damp fresh plaster by mixing pigments with water, sometimes containing lime. At this stage the color integrated permanently with the plaster wall. This method required confidence and sureness of touch because once the color was absorbed into the plaster it was not possible to re-touch.

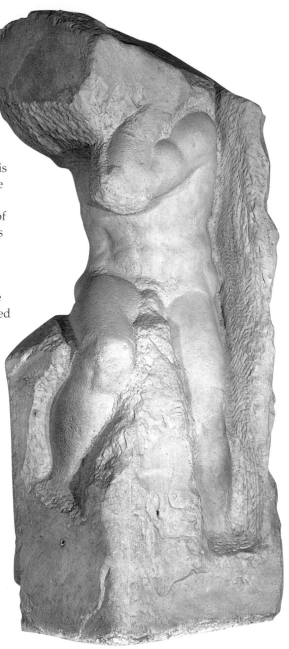

ATLAS

This extraordinary figure of Atlas, carved by Michelangelo in about 1520,demonstrates both the power and technique of his art. Atlas appears to be struggling to free his head from a huge block of stone, and is condemned to do so for all eternity. The figure shows how the artist gradually "frees" the figure by carving into the block.

SIMPLE TOOLS

The hammer and chisel were the means by which Michelangelo created his breathtaking sculptures. The claw chisel (top) dug into the stone, producing a grooved surface as if it had been combed. This type of chiseling action gave the artist greater control and prevented the chisel inadvertently chipping the stone.

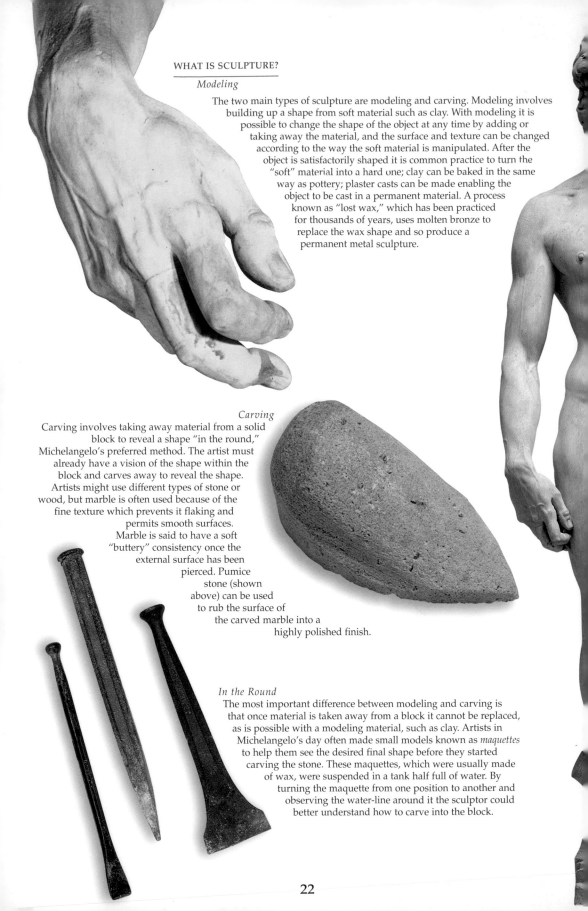

WHAT IS SCULPTURE?

Modeling

The two main types of sculpture are modeling and carving. Modeling involves building up a shape from soft material such as clay. With modeling it is possible to change the shape of the object at any time by adding or taking away the material, and the surface and texture can be changed according to the way the soft material is manipulated. After the object is satisfactorily shaped it is common practice to turn the "soft" material into a hard one; clay can be baked in the same way as pottery; plaster casts can be made enabling the object to be cast in a permanent material. A process known as "lost wax," which has been practiced for thousands of years, uses molten bronze to replace the wax shape and so produce a permanent metal sculpture.

Carving

Carving involves taking away material from a solid block to reveal a shape "in the round," Michelangelo's preferred method. The artist must already have a vision of the shape within the block and carves away to reveal the shape. Artists might use different types of stone or wood, but marble is often used because of the fine texture which prevents it flaking and permits smooth surfaces. Marble is said to have a soft "buttery" consistency once the external surface has been pierced. Pumice stone (shown above) can be used to rub the surface of the carved marble into a highly polished finish.

In the Round

The most important difference between modeling and carving is that once material is taken away from a block it cannot be replaced, as is possible with a modeling material, such as clay. Artists in Michelangelo's day often made small models known as *maquettes* to help them see the desired final shape before they started carving the stone. These maquettes, which were usually made of wax, were suspended in a tank half full of water. By turning the maquette from one position to another and observing the water-line around it the sculptor could better understand how to carve into the block.

THE SCULPTURES

Giorgio Vasari was a Tuscan writer and contemporary of Michelangelo whose book *Lives of the Most Eminent Painters, Sculptors, and Architects*, was first published in 1550. In his account of the life of Michelangelo he quotes the artist as saying that it is no wonder that he took so well to the stonemason's chisel, because as a baby his wet-nurse was the daughter of a stonemason and had married another. Michelangelo thought the milk from the breast influenced him when he grew up. There can be no doubt that Michelangelo is one of the greatest, if not the greatest, sculptor in the history of art. It is reported that when at the age of 26, he started work on the 18 ft (five and a half meter) high block of marble that he was to turn into the figure of *David* he commenced without even making a clay maquette (model) first. Michelangelo built a shed around the block of marble which had lain in a courtyard near the cathedral for nearly a 100 years, abandoned after previous unsuccessful attempts to carve it into a figure by an earlier generation of artists. He had no assistants but attacked the marble with furious energy, sometimes working continuously for several days and nights, not leaving the shed but snatching a few hours sleep on the shed floor.

AWAKENING SLAVE

One of the last pieces worked on by the artist, *The Awakening Slave*, showsMichelangelo's interest in contrasting rough hewn and smooth polished surfaces.

THE PRIDE OF FLORENCE

Michelangelo had already acquired a reputation as a sculptor by the time he made what is perhaps his best known work, the statue of *David*, the boy king, with sling resting on his shoulder. The work is a masterpiece of Renaissance art which demonstrates the idealized human form. The figure stands exactly the height of the original block of marble. The rough surface of the two ends of the block can be seen on the base and crown of *David's* head.

FAMOUS IMAGES

VIRGIN'S HEAD

Some critics have drawn attention to the fact that the Virgin's face has been sculpted in a way that makes her look far too young to be the Mother of Christ. Michelangelo argued that the Virgin could not age because she was so pure. This sculpture, as with all of Michelangelo's work, embodied the idealized human form in the manner of the High Renaissance.

Records show that on November 19, 1497, Jean Bilheres de Lagraulas, a French Cardinal, arranged for Michelangelo to obtain a block of marble from the quarries in Carrara. This was to enable the Cardinal to commission a *Pietà* for his own tomb. This is an early example of a sculpted *Pietà*, which is a representation of the crucified Christ on the lap of his mother. Although the subject was commonly painted in Italy, sculptural representations were more likely to be found in Germany and France. The idea probably originates from Germany in the 14th century and draws a parallel with the Madonna holding the infant Christ on her knee. One of the great problems with this composition is that the figure of Christ has to be at least as large as the Virgin if the proportions are to be realistic, and this leads to difficulties in representing the Virgin properly supporting the dead Christ. Michelangelo completed the sculpture in just one year, but the Cardinal died in August 1499. The *Pietà* was placed over his tomb in St. Peter's, Rome.

THE MADONNA OF THE MEADOW

Giovanni Bellini

This painting, made in about 1500 in Venice, shows the Madonna with the infant Christ on her lap and quite clearly demonstrates the compositional (and religious) parallels with the traditional *Pietà* composition.

PIETÀ

attributed to the Master of Avignon

This depiction of the Pietà was made in Avignon, France, in about 1470, by an unknown artist. It owes more to the Gothic than the Renaissance style with its flat background and artificial decoration around the figures' heads, but it demonstrates the problem of comparative proportion between the Christ and Virgin. In this painting the artist plays on the disparity by bending the figure of the dead Christ across the Virgin's lap, his unsupported legs and head adding to the sense of tragedy and pathos.

It is a measure of Michelangelo's genius that he is able to make the composition realistic without the viewer even questioning the relative proportions of the Virgin and Christ. In fact Michelangelo has cleverly cloaked the Virgin's form in voluminous drapery which disguises the fact that her lap is far too wide and that she would be far taller than her son if she were to stand. None of this matters, however, because the viewer is immediately captured by the pathos evoked by the work. The bowed head of the Virgin, partly cowled by her veil, and the outstretched arm with palm extended is infinitely expressive as she holds her dead son across her lap.

THE AUDIENCE FOR THE PICTURES
THE LAST JUDGEMENT

The Sistine Chapel in Rome was built by Pope Sixtus IV in the 1470s, as part of a building campaign to restore Rome after the papacy moved back there from Avignon. It stands about 131 by 46 ft (40 by 14 meters) wide and originally had windows all around, six on each long wall, two on the altar wall and entrance wall. The Chapel was painted by Michelangelo over a period of years and was completed in 1512. The altar wall originally had frescoes based on the Assumption of the Virgin, Baptism of Christ, and was completed in 1512.

The altar wall originally had frescoes based on the Assumption of the Virgin, Baptism of Christ and Finding of Moses. When Paul III was made Pope in 1534 he commissioned Michelangelo to paint a Last Judgement scene on the altar wall. The two altar wall windows were blocked up and Michelangelo's own frescoes were destroyed along with those by other artists to make room for the new fresco, which would cover the entire wall.

In Michelangelo's painting the figure of Christ in the center with the figure of Mary just behind stands in judgement, holding up his hand to raise the dead ready for their ordeal.

Christ is surrounded by his saints who all protest their sufferings and seek their rewards.

Figures rise from their graves on Christ's right, summoned by trumpeting angels.

The damned fall into Hell on his left, driven on by Charon, the ferryman who takes the dead across the river Styx in his boat.

The Last Judgement reflects the change in fortunes of the Church and of Rome since the original Michelangelo commission to paint the ceiling over 20 years earlier. The apocalyptic painting covers an immense 46 by 39 ft (14 by 12 meters). The invasion and sack of Rome, which probably damaged the original frescoes in the Chapel, and the destructive criticisms of the Church by the Reformation, had served to change the religious mood of the day into a darker and more somber one.

When Sebastiano del Piombo (who was in charge of making the wall ready) had the wall prepared for oil painting, a furious Michelangelo argued that oil painting was fit only for women and lazy people and had the surface removed and prepared again for fresco. When the painting was finally unveiled to Paul III on October 31, 1541, it is said that he fell on his knees praying to God not to remember his sins on Judgement Day.

STORIES FROM THE LAST JUDGEMENT

Pope Paul understood and was supportive of Michelangelo's work but many around him were openly critical of *The Last Judgement*. They said it was obscene and that: *"...the saints and angels, the former without any of the decency proper to this world, and the latter lacking any of the loveliness of Heaven..."* In 1555, the new Pope Paul IV, who had been opposed to *The Last Judgement* painting from the start, asked Michelangelo to make the fresco "suitable." Michelangelo's replied: *"Tell the Pope that this is a small matter and it can easily be made suitable; let him make the world a suitable place and painting will soon follow suit."* Nevertheless shortly after Michelangelo's death the fresco was "made suitable" by the addition of loincloths and other clothes, in some instances irreparably damaging the painting.

THE DAMNED

The judgement condemns the sinners to everlasting damnation in hell. Michelangelo's devils are in human form with only their coloring and claws distinguishing them from the humans they torment. What is so awesome about this vision is the way in which the condemned appear to be resigned to their fate, realizing for the first time that they are doomed and unable to resist. This is brilliantly achieved here by this detail of a man hiding his face and paralyzed with fear, as he is dragged down into hell.

SELF-PORTRAIT

Michelangelo depicts himself as Saint Bartholomew, astride a cloud, below and to the right of the central figure of a youthful Christ. The saints all hold an object symbolizing their martyrdom. Michelangelo holds out his flayed skin, perhaps also as a grim joke about his efforts in the cause of his art.

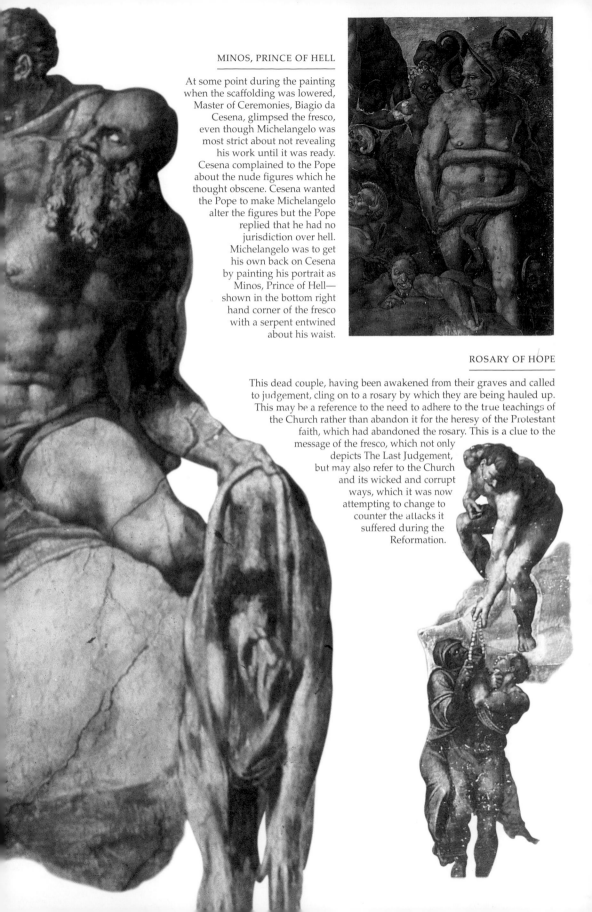

MINOS, PRINCE OF HELL

At some point during the painting when the scaffolding was lowered, Master of Ceremonies, Biagio da Cesena, glimpsed the fresco, even though Michelangelo was most strict about not revealing his work until it was ready. Cesena complained to the Pope about the nude figures which he thought obscene. Cesena wanted the Pope to make Michelangelo alter the figures but the Pope replied that he had no jurisdiction over hell. Michelangelo was to get his own back on Cesena by painting his portrait as Minos, Prince of Hell— shown in the bottom right hand corner of the fresco with a serpent entwined about his waist.

ROSARY OF HOPE

This dead couple, having been awakened from their graves and called to judgement, cling on to a rosary by which they are being hauled up. This may be a reference to the need to adhere to the true teachings of the Church rather than abandon it for the heresy of the Protestant faith, which had abandoned the rosary. This is a clue to the message of the fresco, which not only depicts The Last Judgement, but may also refer to the Church and its wicked and corrupt ways, which it was now attempting to change to counter the attacks it suffered during the Reformation.

THE AUDIENCE FOR THE GREAT WORKS

GOLD FLORIN

Money has always been behind the creation of art.

The power of the great families such as the Medicis was absolute. They had amassed huge fortunes through banking and were very influential in the Church. The Florentine banks of the Medici years became the most important and powerful in Europe and allowed the family to become patrons of artists such as Michelangelo and Leonardo da Vinci, favorites of Lorenzo "the Magnificent" Medici. The Church was also enormously powerful, having been re-established in Rome. Its leading figures such as Pope Julius II, were concerned with building the image of the Church. Julius II supported the Medicis of Florence, and encouraged Florentine artists such as Michelangelo to work on the new projects he was planning for Rome. Julius II commissioned Bramante to build the Church of St. Peter's which was to dominate the architecture of the city. The work of the great artists served to reinforce the power of the Church and its messages to a population whose life was centered on religion.

POPE JULIUS II *Raphael*

When Michelangelo had completed the Sistine Chapel ceiling frescoes for Pope Julius II, they were admired by all of Rome, whose people came crowding to see the spectacular sight. Julius considered that the paintings might be improved a little: *"It must still be necessary to have it re-touched with gold"* was his comment, according to Vasari's book. Michelangelo's reply was: *"I do not see that men should wear gold."* The Pope continued: "It will look poor." Michelangelo answered by saying: *"Those who are painted here were poor themselves."*

THE LIFE OF MICHELANGELO

~1505~
Traveled to Rome to undertake a commission for Pope Julius II's tomb. A change of plan and Michelangelo is asked to paint the ceiling of the Sistine Chapel

~1512~
Sistine Chapel finished and unveiled

~1518~
Commissioned by Pope Leo to design the facade of the Medici family church of San Lorenzo in Florence but the work was abandoned as money ran out

~1524~
Designed and executed the Medici tombs

~1527~
War in Rome as the Medicis were forced to flee and troops rampaged through the city. Michelangelo returned to Florence. His brother died of the plague

~1531~
Michelangelo's father died

~1535~
Michelangelo appointed sculptor and architect to the Pope

~1536~
Met Vittoria Colonna, the Marchioness of Pescara. They remained close until her death

~1547~
Appointed architect of St. Peter's in Rome

~1564~
Michelangelo died on February 18.

THE DONI TONDO

Circular paintings became popular in Italy in the 15th century (Tondo is Italian for round); this one was commissioned by the Doni family in 1503. It depicts the Holy Family, with Mary reaching over her shoulder to take the infant Christ from Joseph. Michelangelo was asked to make the Tondo for the wedding of Agnolo Doni and Maddalena Strozzi. It is said that when the painting was delivered, Agnolo Doni tried to settle for paying 40 ducats rather than the 70 ducats earlier agreed. Michelangelo threatened to take the painting back unless Doni paid twice the original sum, to which he eventually agreed.

PORTRAIT OF COSIMO DE'MEDICI

Pontormo

From 1434, Cosimo started to create his empire in Florence, constructing public buildings and commissioning artists. Lorenzo continued the family tradition when he came to power in 1469, six years before the birth of Michelangelo.

WHAT THE CRITICS SAY

One story has it that Michelangelo's rivals Bramante and Raphael conspired to get Michelangelo the commission for the Sistine Chapel frescoes knowing that he would refuse, as he considered himself a sculptor not a painter, and thereby earn the disapproval of the Pope and so be out of favor. How true this is we do not know, but this work is a lasting legacy upon which art historians and critics have heaped praise for centuries. Michelangelo is acknowledged as being instrumental in bringing about a change in the course of art. Not content with learning the techniques of art as a young apprentice, he strived to understand fully the complexity of the subject that fascinated him most: the human body. He even dissected corpses to be able to appreciate and represent the human form in any position or pose. This mastery earned him fame and wealth as rich merchants and Popes competed for his services but it also elevated paintings and sculptures from the status of crafts to "fine arts." Many historians credit Michelangelo with being the greatest sculptor, painter, and draughtsman ever; he is an archetype of the artist as genius.

FAME IN PRINT

"From the hour when the Lord God, by His outstanding kindness, made me worthy not just of the presence (which I could scarcely have hoped to enter), but of the love, of the conversation, and of the intimacy of Michelangelo Buonarroti, the unique sculptor and painter..."
so begins Vasari's uncritical biography of Michelangelo, and so begins the legend of Michelangelo, the genius.
Unlike any artist before him, Michelangelo was the subject of two biographies in his lifetime.
Giorgio Vasari (shown above) published his *Lives of the Most Eminent Painters, Sculptors, and Architects* book in 1550, when Michelangelo was 75 years old. Three years later Ascanio Condivi published his *"Life of Michelangelo."* The legend began in his lifetime and has continued for nearly 500 years.

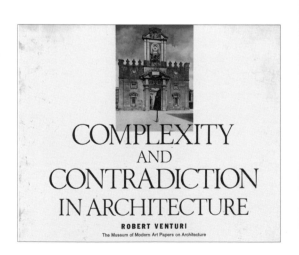

Today students and critics refer back to the inventions of Michelangelo as one of the major influences on the course of Western architecture.

FAME IN STONE

Pope Julius II had commissioned the architect Bramante to build a new church of St. Peter's in Rome. When Bramante died in 1514 the church was unfinished, and he left no plans or models for its completion. Bramante's successors made no progress and Michelangelo was asked by Pope Paul III to take over the project in 1547. Michelangelo agreed to do it without payment for his "spiritual good." He rejected the design of his predecessor, Sangallo, and came up with his own which he said was more faithful to Bramante's original (despite the fact that he and Bramante had been enemies), criticizing Sangallo's design as: *"providing pasturage for sheep and oxen who know nothing of art."* In return Sangallo's supporters criticized Michelangelo to such an extent that the Pope had to intervene.

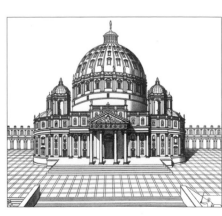

Michelangelo planned a hemispherical dome, as the drawings show. Building started in the late 1550s and halted on Michelangelo's death in 1564. The drum upon which the dome sits is by Michelangelo's hand, but the dome's shape was changed by his successor, della Porta, who considered the hemisphere to lack stability and changed it to the more pointed shape that we see today.

THE CENTER OF POWER

The power of
Michelangelo's influence on
artists of later generations
is exemplified by a quote
from the 20th century
Russian Suprematist artist,
Kasimir Malevich. Malevich
was among the first
painters to work in a
completely abstract idiom.
He strived to achieve "the
supremacy of pure feeling."
To Malevich, the object was
meaningless and the ideas
of the conscious mind
worthless. He said that the
point at which the apex of
a triangle touched the
circumference of a circle
was visually as powerful as
the gap between the hand
of God and the hand of
Adam from Michelangelo's
Creation of Adam.
Malevich was recognizing
the compositional power of
Michelangelo's art and
trying to achieve it in his
own, in purely abstract
terms. The above painting:
*M. Matuischin by Kazimir
Malevich (1878-1935)*

A LASTING IMPRESSION

Michelangelo's influence on the course of Western art and architecture
has been profound. The challenge of drawing the naked human form
in complicated poses persists as a test for the would-be artist even
today. The strength of Michelangelo's work lies in its ability to
understand, imitate, and even surpass the classical masters and to
build on this by following his own spirit of invention. By influencing
Italian art he influenced European art, and thereby art of the Western
world. His buildings still dominate Rome today and his sculptures
and paintings are monumental milestones in the course of the history
of art. Michelangelo considered himself to be a sculptor above all
else. He believed his chisels released the sculpture from the stone.
This famous sonnet was written in reply to Giovanni Strozzi who said
that: *the sculpture of Night for the Medici chapel tomb of Giuliano
de'Medici was sculpted by an angel and would speak if awoken!*

> *"Caro m'e 'l sonno...*
> *Dear to me is sleep*
> *in stone while harm*
> *and shame persist;*
> *not to see, not to feel, is bliss;*
> *speak softly, do not wake me,*
> *do not weep."*

This detail from the *Creation of Adam* has been used
time and time again for all kinds of purposes such
as advertising, films, television, and graphics. This
is a testimony to its fame and everlasting endurance
as an icon of 500 years standing.

During the latter part of his life, and continuing after his death, artists painting in the style of Michelangelo crowded their paintings with naked athletes. These pictures in the manner of Michelangelo imitated his style but missed the spirit of his work. This fashion has today became known as "Mannerism." The fashion tended to elongate the human form, depicting it as a classical ideal, representing the figures in standard poses and portraying faces vacant of meaningful expression. Mannerist painters use intense colors to heighten emotional effect and the drama of the scene. El Greco was one of the most famous "Mannerist" painters.

The Trinity, El Greco.

THE HEART OF ROME

The site of the Capitoline Hill was the civic center of ancient Rome, run down and medieval in appearance at the time of Michelangelo. Pope Paul III's plans to restore the site, known as the Piazza del Campidoglio, involved Michelangelo's designs for a re-modeled square. The scheme was not finished until almost 100 years after Michelangelo's death but is today a magnet for visitors to Rome. Its design reflects the ancient Roman tradition of *caput mundi*, the center of the world.

DID YOU KNOW?
FASCINATING FACTS ABOUT THE ARTIST
AND THE TIMES IN WHICH HE WORKED

• Michelangelo spent so long painting the Sistine Chapel ceiling with his head turned upward, that for a long time afterward he couldn't adjust to looking down again and he had to read things by holding them over his head. He described the misery of this in a poem.

• In preparation for the Sistine Chapel ceiling, he made about 300 preliminary drawings.

• "Buon fresco" or "true fresco," describes painting on wet plaster so that pigment bonds with the actual wall or ceiling.

• Originally, Michelangelo was going to paint the twelve Apostles (from the New Testament) on the ceiling, but he ended up painting more than 300 life-sized figures instead.

• Most Renaissance artists used assistants to paint some of their pictures, but Michelangelo painted the 44 yard long, 15 yard wide ceiling nearly all by himself over four years.

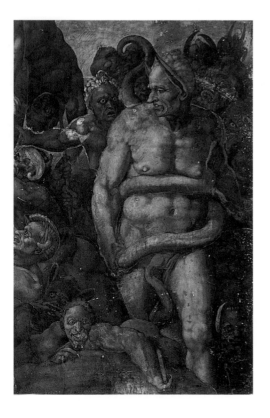

• In 1536, Michelangelo was appointed to design the Capitoline Hill; one of the seven hills of Rome. His symmetrical and harmonious design included a piazza and a palace.

• Pope Julius II commissioned him to create a magnificent tomb. Michelangelo worked on it for over forty years, originally planning to include forty bronze statues, but Julius postponed the work. After the pope's death, Michelangelo's instructions changed several times and the scale of the tomb was drastically reduced. Michelangelo declared that the tomb robbed him of his youth.

Discussed widely since he first created them, Michelangelo's Slaves were originally intended for Pope Julius II's tomb, but no one knows exactly what they represent. Michelangelo called them *prigioni*, which means captives. One appears calm and patient, while the other is agitated and restless.

• When he was a young sculptor in Rome it is said that Michelangelo overheard some people saying his new *Pietà* in St. Peter's Basilica was by another artist. He was so cross that he returned to the church at night and on Mary's sash carved the words "Michelangelo Buonarroti, Florentine, made this." It was the only work he ever signed.

• For most of his life, Michelangelo had a misshapen nose! It happened when he argued with another artist called Pietro Torrigiani who punched him on the nose and broke it.

• He deliberately carved his huge statue of David out of proportion. David's hands, head, and upper body are larger than the lower body. He knew that when the statue was high up, the proportions would appear correct to onlookers below.

- The statue of David came from the Old Testament story of the boy who killed a giant, with just a stone in a sling. This was to symbolize the strength of the City of Florence against the bigger and more powerful forces around it.

- A member of the Florentine government said he thought David's nose was too large. The normally arrogant Michelangelo quietly climbed up the scaffolding and chiseled away at the nose. Marble dust fell to the ground below and the member of the government said the nose was now perfect. But Michelangelo had only pretended to chisel, sprinkling marble dust from his pocket. He didn't actually change David's nose at all.

- Michelangelo (and other artists of the time) did not use female models, so all his figures were drawn from male models—probably his young apprentices. He was not particularly interested in making his females look feminine anyway.

- At the age of 72, Michelangelo was commissioned as architect of St. Peter's Basilica in Rome. Using his many skills, he concentrated especially on the dome, which was to stand directly over the grave of St. Peter, but when he died, building work was still not finished. It was completed twenty-six years later by two other architects.

- A year after Michelangelo's death, another artist, Daniele da Volterra, was paid by Church authorities to paint clothes over nude figures in his *The Last Judgement* fresco in the Sistine Chapel. It earned da Volterra the nickname "Il Braghettone" ("the breeches-maker").

- It took restorers twenty years to renovate the ceiling of the Sistine Chapel—more than twice as long as it took Michelangelo to paint it!

SUMMARY TIMELINE OF
THE ARTIST & HIS CONTEMPORARIES

THE LIFE OF MICHELANGELO

~1475~
Giovanni de' Medici, the future Pope Leo X is born in the same year as Michelangelo

~1476~
The Sicilian artist Antonello da Messina paints *Virgin Annunciate*

~1479~
da Messina dies

~1483~
Raphael is born

~1484~
Botticelli paints one of his masterpieces, *The Birth of Venus*

~1485~
Michelangelo's widowed father marries again and the family moves to Florence; the War of the Roses in England ends

~1488~
The artist Tiziano Vecellio, later known as Titian, is born

~1490-1500~
The Venetian Renaissance artist Giovanni Bellini paints *Madonna and Child with Saints*

~1492~
Christopher Columbus sails across the Atlantic Ocean, ending up in the Americas; the artist Piero della Francesca and Lorenzo de' Medici die

~1494~
The artist Jacopo Pontormo is born; Hans Memling, German-born Flemish artist and Ghirlandaio die

~1497~
The Italian navigator and explorer Giovanni Caboto, known in English as John Cabot, reaches North America; Hans Holbein the Younger is born in Bavaria

~1500~
The Italian artist Giorgione paints *The Holy Family*; canvas is used as a support for painting for the first time; the Italian artist Benvenuto Cellini is born

~1501~
Amerigo Vespucci discovers and names All Saints' Bay in Brazil; Michelangelo is commissioned to create *David*; as a symbol of

Florence's strength against powerful enemies

~1503~
The Mannerist artist, Girolamo Francesco Maria Mazzola, later known as Parmigianino, is born

~1503-1506~
Leonardo paints the *Mona Lisa*

~1506~
The Northern Italian Renaissance artist Andrea Mantegna dies

~1508~
Raphael begins painting the Vatican chambers while Michelangelo is painting the Sistine Chapel ceiling nearby

~1509~
Henry VIII becomes King of England; an earthquake in Constantinople kills 13000 people

~1510~
Giorgione and Botticelli die

~1512~
The completed Sistine Chapel ceiling is shown to the public for the first time; Michelangelo buys two houses in Florence

~1513~
Pope Julius II dies, Pope
Leo X succeeds him and
a new contract for Julius'
tomb is drawn up

~1515~
François I is crowned
King of France

~1516~
Another contract is drawn up
for Michelangelo's work on
Julius' tomb; Bellini dies

~1518~
Tintoretto, one of the greatest
painters of the Venetian
School, is born

~1519~
Leonardo dies in France

~1520~
Raphael dies; Suleiman I "the
Magnificent" becomes Sultan
of the Ottoman Empire

~1525~
Santa Marta, the first city in
Colombia, is founded by
Spanish conqueror Rodrigo
de Bastidas; the great
Flemish artist, Pieter Bruegel
the Elder is born

~1527~
The artist Giuseppe
Arcimboldo is born

~1528~
The German artist Albrecht
Dürer dies; Pietro Torrigiano,
the artist who broke
Michelangelo's nose dies; the
Mayan people drive Spanish
Conquistadores out of Yucatán;
Michelangelo works on the
fortifications of Florence

~1529~
Vienna is besieged by the
Turkish forces of Suleiman

~1530s~
Titian paints *Madonna and
Child with a Female Saint and
the Infant Saint John the Baptist*

~1531~
Lisbon, Portugal is hit by an
earthquake killing millions;
a comet is seen, named nearly
170 years later, as Halley's

~1532~
Michelangelo meets
Tommaso Cavalieri who
becomes his close friend

~1533~
Henry VIII marries
Anne Boleyn

~1536~
In England, Catherine of
Aragon dies and Anne Boleyn
is executed; Michelangelo
begins work on *The Last
Judgement* on the altar wall
of the Sistine Chapel in
Vatican City—it takes him
four years to complete

~1537~
Michelangelo is made an
honorary citizen of Rome

~1541~
El Greco is born in Crete,
but later moves to Spain
and becomes one of the
greatest Mannerist painters;
the Spanish explorer Hernando
de Soto reaches the Mississippi
River and names it the
Rio de Espiritu Santo
("River of the Holy Spirit")

~1547~
Michelangelo is named
architect of St. Peter's in Rome

~1550~
Michelangelo completes his
fresco The Last Judgement

~1555~
Michelangelo, becoming
increasingly religious, turns
his attention from painting
and sculpture toward more
architectural projects to serve
the Church. His assistant,
Francesco Urbino dies

~1556~
The Shaanxi Earthquake,
the deadliest earthquake
in history, occurs in China:
it is believed that 830,000
people are killed

~1558~
Elizabeth I ascends the
throne of England

~1564~
Michelangelo dies at 88 years
old; he is buried in the church
of Santa Croce in Florence;
William Shakespeare is born

WHAT DID HE SAY?

Here are some of the things that Michelangelo said or wrote that have been passed down to us:

• "A man paints with his brains and not with his hands"

• "…for twelve years now I have gone about all over Italy, leading a miserable life; I have borne every kind of humiliation, suffered every kind of hardship, worn myself to the bone…solely to help my family"

• "I saw the angel in the marble and carved until I set him free"

• "In every block of marble I see a statue as plain as though it stood before me, shaped and perfect in attitude and action. I have only to hew away the rough walls that imprison the lovely apparition to reveal it to the other eyes as mine see it"

• "Genius is eternal patience"

• "Every block of stone has a statue inside it and it is the task of the sculptor to discover it"

• "The greater danger for most of us lies not in setting our aim too high and falling short; but in setting our aim too low, and achieving our mark"

• "What spirit is so empty and blind, that it cannot recognize the fact that the foot is nobler than the shoe and skin more beautiful than the garment with which it is clothed?"

• "I've got myself a goitre from this strain…
My beard towards heaven, I feel the back of my brain
Upon my neck, I grow the breast of a harpy;
My brush above my face continually…"

A WORK IN CLOSE-UP

The Sistine Chapel ceiling was originally painted blue with gold stars—the traditional way for a church ceiling to be painted—and nobody knows why Pope Julius II asked Michelangelo to change it. As with many of the images on this ceiling, the Creation of Eve is from a story in the Old Testament. Michelangelo painted it in the center of the ceiling, next to other linking stories from the Bible. This is the story of how God made the first woman from one of Adam's ribs. The composition was inspired by the relief panels that surround the door of the Basilica of San Petronio in Bologna by Jacopo della Quercia whose work Michelangelo studied when he was younger.

The Creation of Eve, 1508-12, fresco, 67 x 102 in/170 x 260 cm, *Sistine Chapel, Vatican, Rome, Italy*

God is standing to the right of the picture, looking tall, wise and dignified, swathed in a violet cloak over his red tunic. He bends toward Eve, his hand raised in a welcoming gesture.

Eve, portrayed as a young woman, is rising from the rocks where God has made her. Hands together in prayer, she bends toward him, thanking him for her creation. Her figure makes a diagonal link between God and the sleeping figure of Adam.

Meanwhile, Adam sleeps on, unaware of what is happening. His horizontal head and body are supported by the trunk of a tree with branches that extend in the shape of a cross—a reference to the crucifixion of Jesus in the New Testament.

WHERE TO SEE THIS ARTIST'S WORKS IN THE USA

The most important artworks by Michelangelo are mainly in Italy, but you can still see some of his drawings and preparatory work in the USA. Always check before visiting that the work is on display.

Detroit Institute of Arts, Michigan
(www.dia.org)

The Getty Museum, Los Angeles
(www.getty.edu)

The Metropolitan Museum, New York
(www.metmuseum.org)

Cleveland Museum of Art, Ohio
(www.clemusart.com)

Frick Collection, New York
(www.frick.org)

Harvard University Art Museums, Massachusetts
(www.artmuseums. harvard.edu)

Kimbell Art Museum, *Texas (www.kimbellart.org)*

WHERE TO SEE THIS ARTIST'S
WORKS IN THE REST OF THE WORLD

Most of Michelangelo's major works are still in Italy, especially his buildings and sculpture, but you can also see some of his work in other countries, mainly in Europe:

Sistine Chapel,
Vatican City,
Italy

St. Peter's Basilica,
Vatican City, Italy
*(http://mv.vatican.va/
3_EN/pages/CSN/
CSN_Main.html)*

Casa Buonarroti,
Florence, Italy
(www.casabuonarroti.it)

Medici Chapel,
San Lorenzo, Florence, Italy
**(www.museumsinflorence.c
om/musei/Medici_chapels)**

Galleria dell'Accademia,
Florence, Italy
*(www.polomuseale.
firenze.it/accademia)*

Santo Spirito,
Florence, Italy

**Museo Nazionale
del Bargello,**
Florence, Italy
*(www.polomuseale.firenze.it/e
nglish/musei/bargello)*

Palazzo Vecchio,
Florence, Italy
*(www.museumsinflorence.
com/musei/Palazzo_vecchio)*

**Museo dell'Opera
del Duomo,**
Florence, Italy

Uffizi Gallery,
Florence, Italy
(www.uffizi.com)

Castello Sforzesco,
Milan, Italy

San Domenico,
Bologna, Italy

Church of Our Lady,
Bruges, Belgium
Louvre, Paris, France
(www.louvre.fr)

The Royal Collection,
London, UK
*(www.royalcollection.
org.uk)*

Royal Academy of Arts,
London, UK
(www.racollection.org.uk)

National Gallery,
London, UK
*(www.nationalgallery.
org.uk)*

State Hermitage Museum,
St. Petersburg, Russia
*(www.hermitage
museum.org)*

FURTHER READING & WEBSITES

BOOKS

Michelangelo:
Sculptor and Painter
(Signature Lives:
Renaissance Era),
Barbara A. Somervill,
Compass Point Books, 2008

Michelangelo Buonarroti
(The Life & Work of...),
Sean Connolly,
Heinemann Library, 2007

Michelangelo: Painter,
Sculptor, and Architect,
Tim McNeese,
Chelsea House Publishers,
2005

Michelangelo
(Culture in Action),
Jane Bingham,
Raintree, 2009

Michelangelo
(QED Great Lives),
Philip Wilkinson,
QED Publishing, 2006

Michelangelo
(First Impressions),
Richard B. K. McLanathan,
Harry N. Abrams, Inc, 1993

Michelangelo
(Artists and their Works),
Shelley Swanson Sateren,
Bridgestone Books, 2002

Michelangelo
(Great Names),
Diane Cook,
Mason Crest Publishers, 2002

The Essential
Michelangelo, Klaus
Ottmann,
Harry N. Abrams, Inc, 2000

Michelangelo,
Diane Stanley,
HarperCollins Publishers,
2003

Art at the Time
of Michelangelo,
Antony Mason,
Franklin Watts Publishing,
2001

Tudor Art (Art in History),
Susie Hodge,
Heinemann Library, 2006

Art on the Wall:
The Renaissance,
Richard Spilsbury,
Heinemann Library, 2009

Renaissance
(Eyewitness Art),
Alison Ambrose,
Dorling Kindersley
Publishers Ltd, 1998

WEBSITES

www.michelangelo.com/
buonarroti

www.artchive.com/
artchive/M/michelangelo

www.ibiblio.org/wm/
paint/auth/michelangelo/

www.wga.hu/frames-
e.html?/bio/m/michelan/
biograph

www.bbc.co.uk/history/hist
oric_figures/michelangelo

www.artsmarts4kids.blogs
pot.com/2007/09/
michelangelos-sistine-
chapel-ceiling.html

www.kyrene.k12.az.us/
schools/brisas/sunda/
art/michelang.htm

www.mega.it/eng/egui/
pers/micbuon.htm

www.yesnet.yk.ca/schools/
projects/renaissance/
michelangelo.html

www.moodbook.com/
history/renaissance/
sistine-chapel.html

www.library.thinkquest.
org/21960/tqs310.htm

www.wga.hu/frames-
e.html?/html/m/michelan/
3sistina/index.html

45

GLOSSARY

Apprentice—young people who learn a trade or craft under the guidance of a skilled person

Architecture—the design and construction of buildings

Classical—generally describes a type of art and design derived from the examples and styles of ancient Greece and Rome. Art and design from these early examples were thought to be of the highest quality

Commission—to order something and pay for it

Fresco—from the Italian word for "fresh," frescoes are paintings made on damp plaster. Fresco artists must work quickly and accurately on small areas of wet plaster so that the paint becomes part of the plaster

Gothic—usually describes an architectural style that developed between the twelfth and sixteenth centuries in Northern Europe, although it sometimes refers to other art forms too. The style is tall, thin and decorative

Mannerism—a term we use today to describe some types of art that followed

the Renaissance which broke the rules of classical art. Mannerist painters often elongated the human form and used vivid colors to emphasize emotion

Pantheon—a circular temple in Rome based on earlier Greek temple designs, dedicated to the ancient Roman gods. Originally built in 27BC, it was later rebuilt and used for Christian worship

Pigment—colored powder that is mixed with other substances, such as oil, water, or egg, to make paint

Polymath—a person skilled in many different areas

Proportion—how the measurements of objects relate to the other parts. For instance, in the human body, an adult human head is about one-seventh of the height of the figure

Renaissance—a word that means "rebirth" and came to be used during the nineteenth century to describe the interest in classical art and learning that occurred from about 1400 to 1520

INDEX

ACKNOWLEDGMENTS

Picture Credits t=top, b=bottom, c=center, l=left, r=right, OFC=outside front cover.

Photo © AKG London/Erich Lessing; 10tl. © Ancient Art & Architecture Collection; 6/7cb, 18tr. Ashmolean Museum, Oxford; 13tl. Ashmolean Museum, University of Oxford/The Bridgeman Art Library; OFCt. Bargello, Florence/Bridgeman Art Library, London; 30tl. Copyright © British Museum; 19cb. Collegium Maius, Cracow, Poland. Photo © AKG London/Erich Lessing; 7br. Cappella Medici, Florence/Bridgeman Art Library, London; 18br, 19tr. Casa Buonarroti, Florence/Bridgeman Art Library, London; 5. Mary Evans Picture Library; 6bl, 7tr, 32tl. Galleria degli Uffizi, Florence. Photo © AKG London/Erich Lessing; 11br, 31cb. Galleria degli Uffizi, Florence/Bridgeman Art Library, London; 12bl, 31tl. Galleria dell'Accademia, Florence/Alinari/The Bridgeman Art Library; OFC (main image); Galleria dell'Accademia, Florence. Photo © AKG London; 7c. Galleria dell'Accademia, Florence. Photo © AKG London/Erich Lessing; 22/23c. Galleria dell'Accademia, Florence/Bridgeman Art Library, London; 9cb, 22tl, 23tr, 23br. Galleria dell'Accademia, Florence/Lauros-Giraudon/Bridgeman Art Library, London; 21tr. Chris Gray; 9tl, 32/33cb, 34/35cb. Kunsthistorisches Museum, Vienna. Photo © AKG London/Erich Lessing; 9tr. Musee du Louvre, Paris. Photo © AKG London/Erich Lessing; 11cl, 25tr. Museo dell'Opera del Duomo, Florence. Photo © AKG London/Erich Lessing; 12tl. Museum fur Volkerkunde, Berlin/Bridgeman Art Library, London; 6tl. By courtesy of the Trustees of The National Gallery, London; 24bl. National Gallery, London. Photo © AKG London; 30bl. National Maritime Museum, London; 7tl. Palazzo Medici-Riccardi, Florence. Photo © AKG London; 8bl. Private Collection/Bridgeman Art Library, London; 34tl. Prado, Madrid/Bridgeman Art Library, London; OFCb, 35tr. © Ronald Sheridan/Ancient Art & Architecture Collection; 33t. Sistine Chapel, Vatican, Rome. Photo © AKG London; 26/27. St. Peter's, Vatican/Bridgeman Art Library, London; 24/25c. Stanza della Segnatura, Vatican, Rome. Photo © AKG London/Erich Lessing; 11tr. Unterlindenmuseum, Colmar. Photo © AKG London/Erich Lessing; 10bl. Vatican Museums and Galleries, Rome/Bridgeman Art Library, London; OFCc, 13cb, 14/15, 16t & 34cr, 16/17cb, 17tr, 28tl, 28/29c, 29tr, 29br.

NOTE TO READERS
The website addresses are correct at the time of publishing. However, due to the ever-changing nature of the Internet, websites and content may change. Some websites can contain links that are unsuitable for children. The publisher is not responsible for changes in content or website addresses. We advise that Internet searches should be supervised by an adult.